W9-ATL-701

MITTENS

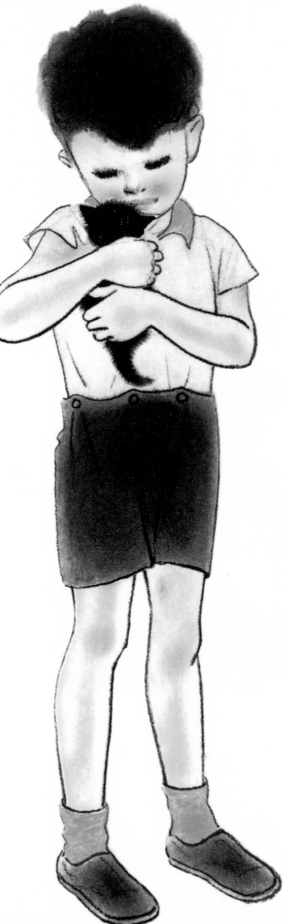

Copyright © 1936 by Clare Turlay Newberry
Copyright renewed 1963 by Clare Newberry

First SMITHMARK edition, 1998

All rights reserved. No part of this publication may be reproduced,
stored in a retrieval system or transmitted in any form by any means
electronic, mechanical, photocopying or otherwise without first obtaining
written permission from the publisher.

This edition published in 1998 by SMITHMARK Publishers, a division of
U.S. Media Holdings, Inc., 115 West 18th Street, New York, NY 10011.

SMITHMARK books are available for bulk purchase for sales promotion
and premium use. For details write or call the manager of special sales,
SMITHMARK Publishers, 115 West 18th Street, New York, NY 10011;
212-519-1300.

Library of Congress Catalog Card Number: 97-62211
ISBN: 0–7651–9059–1

Printed in Hong Kong
10 9 8 7 6 5 4 3 2 1

MITTENS

Story and Pictures by
CLARE TURLAY NEWBERRY

SMITHMARK

To
Richard Stephen Newberry

MITTENS

ONCE there was a little boy named Richard who loved cats and kittens. He talked to all the cats he met on the street, and every day he said to his mother:

"Mother, I want a kitten. *Why* can't I have a kitten?"

"Because you are too little, Richard," his mother would answer. "When you are older you may have one."

So Richard had to wait, but he kept on asking, just the same. And every day he grew older and bigger.

One Saturday he went with his mother to the Farmers' Market

to buy a chicken for Sunday. And there, in a booth along with butter and eggs and cottage cheese, was the cutest kitten he had ever seen. It was a fat tabby kitten, in a chicken-wire cage, and when he saw Richard he opened his little pink mouth and said, "Mew?"

"Mother," said Richard, tugging at her sleeve, "look!"

Richard's mother looked at the kitten, and the kitten looked back at her.

"Mew?" he said again. Then he got up and rubbed his head against the side of the cage and began to purr.

"Goodness! what a loud purr for such a small kitten!" said Richard's mother, and she reached a finger through the wire and petted his nose.

"Mother," begged Richard, "I want that kitten. Please, Mother."

"Now, Richard—" said his mother, and he just knew what was coming next.

"Mother, listen," he urged. "I'm almost six years old and I wear size seven suits. Surely I'm big enough now. *Please*, Mother!"

"Well, I don't know," said his mother, uncertainly.

"He's only twenty-five cents," said the farm woman behind the counter. "And see," she added, pointing to his feet, "he's got mitten paws."

"*Mitten* paws?" said Richard. "What are they?"

"He has six toes on each front paw, instead of only five," explained the woman, "and they make his paws look like mittens." And indeed they did look exactly like mittens—little fur mittens. That settled it for Richard.

"Just think, Mother," he said, earnestly, "he's even got mitten paws! We've just *got* to have him!"

"Well, all right, then," said his mother, weakening. And she paid the woman a quarter out of her purse.

"Hooray! hooray! hooray!" cried Richard, jumping up and down. "Thank you, Mother, thank you!"

So the farm woman put the kitten into a paper bag with just his head and front paws sticking out. She handed him to Richard, who held him very carefully in both hands, like a bag of hot popcorn.

"I know what to name him, Mother," said Richard as they walked to the car, "I just now thought of it—*Mittens!*"

When they got home Mittens had some warm milk — in a jar-top because that was the only thing small enough for him. When he had lapped it all up with his little pink tongue he gave himself a thorough washing. After that he climbed up into an armchair and went to sleep.

Next morning Richard was awakened by a "purr-purr purr-purr" from the foot of his bed. There was Mittens, purring away like anything and kneading his mitten paws up and down on the blanket, the way kittens do when they are friendly.

"Hi, Mittens!" said Richard, rolling out of bed. He began to dress in a hurry so as to have time to play awhile before breakfast. But Mittens couldn't wait—he began to play a little game of his own that he had just thought up. He hid under the bed and pretended he wasn't there. Then suddenly he pounced out and

grabbed one of Richard's bare feet.

"Ow!" said Richard. "Mittens, stop it! Let *go!*"

But Mittens just held on tightly with his front feet and kicked hard with his hind ones. He was pretending Richard's foot was an enemy he was being very fierce with. Then all at once he stopped kicking and began to lick Richard's toes, to show that he was only playing and hadn't meant to hurt.

One afternoon Aunt Evie came to call on Richard's mother. She brought Norine along with her. Norine was the kind of baby that was just big enough to toddle around and grab things. When she saw Mittens she squealed, "Kit-ty, kit-ty!" and picked him up by the tail and *squeezed* him. So of course he scratched her.

"Wow!" shrieked Norine, dropping Mittens and running to her mother.

"Precious lamb!" cried Aunt Evie, and she kissed the scratched arm to make it well, and said that she thought kittens were dangerous for children. Richard's mother said *she* thought children were even more dangerous for kittens. Then Aunt Evie and Norine went home.

"Come on out, Mittens," called Richard, looking under the sofa. "Norine has gone home and nobody will pull your tail now."

But Mittens was not under the sofa.

"Maybe he went upstairs," said Richard's mother, so he ran up to see. But Mittens wasn't upstairs, either.

They looked under the beds, and in the clothes-closet, and behind the doors, and even in the gas-oven and the ice-box, be-

cause you never know about kittens. But they couldn't find Mittens anywhere.

At last Richard's mother said, "Darling, I'm afraid your kitten has gotten out. The delivery boy may have let him out when he brought in the groceries. Put on your coat and we'll look around outside."

So they looked around outside. And they called, "He-re, Mitty-Mitty-Mitty! He-re, Mitty-Mitty-Mitty!" until their throats hurt. But they couldn't find him anywhere.

Richard's mother asked all the neighbors, "Have you seen a little gray tabby kitten, about so big?" and all the neighbors said, "No, we haven't, but we certainly will let you know if we do."

When Richard's father came home to dinner there was no one to meet him at the front door. Richard was crying in the living-room, and his mother was wandering around in the basement, peering into all the dark corners and calling, "He-re, Mitty-Mitty-Mitty!"

"For Heaven's sake," said his father, "what's all this about?"

"Oh, Daddy!" sobbed Richard, "I've l-lost my k-kitten!"

"Lost your kitten?" said his father, "Lost Mittens? How did that happen?"

Just then his mother came up from the basement with cobwebs in her hair, and she told him all about it.

"Something must be done about this," said Richard's father, and he strode across the room to the telephone. He called up the

daily newspaper and told them to print in tomorrow's paper that Mittens was lost.

After that they all felt better and Richard stopped crying. And he and his father helped get dinner because his mother had been so busy hunting for Mittens that she had not even started to peel the potatoes.

The next morning the newspaper had printed just what Richard's father had told them to. It was in the LOST AND FOUND part of the paper, and this is what it said:

"Lost: black-and-gray tabby kitten. Child's pet. REWARD." And after that came Richard's address and telephone number.

"How soon do you think they will bring Mittens back, Daddy?" asked Richard at the breakfast table.

"I don't know, son," said his father, as he started off to work. "It might be any minute now."

So Richard sat down near the front door to wait. And pretty soon the doorbell went *brrrrrrrrrr!* Richard shouted, "Moth-er!" and flung open the door.

There stood a boy with a cat in his arms. But it was not Mittens —oh, my, no! It was a big old yellow tomcat with raggedy ears and a mean look in his eyes.

"Hello, kid!" grinned the boy. "Here's your cat. I found him. How about that reward?"

"But that cat's not Mittens!" exclaimed Richard.

"No, indeed, that's not Mittens!" said his mother, coming to the door. "Mittens was a very tiny kitten."

"But, gee, lady," said the boy, "this is a swell cat! He fights dogs. Maybe your Mittens grew. Are you sure this ain't him?"

"Quite sure," said Richard's mother. So the boy said, "O. K., lady," and ran down the steps.

"Oh, mother," said Richard, "I thought that would be Mittens."

"I'm sorry, darling," said his mother, "but don't cry. It's still very early in the morning. Perhaps there will be another answer to our advertisement."

Just then the phone went *zzzzzzzzzzzzing!* and she hurried to answer it.

A lady at the other end of town wanted to know if Richard's mother would like to buy some white Persian kittens with blue eyes and long pedigrees. Richard's mother didn't, so the lady hung up.

And then the doorbell went *brrrrrrrrrrr!* again. This time it was an old lady with a large lumpy shopping-bag under her arm.

"Good morning, little boy," she greeted Richard, sweetly, "I've a surprise for you—I've found your lost pussy-cat." And she reached into her big bag and pulled out—a little, scared, *black* kitten.

"Oh dear! that isn't Mittens, either!" said Richard.

"Oh no, that isn't our cat," said his mother. "Ours was a gray tabby kitten."

"Well, now, that's a shame," said the old lady. "But why don't you let the little chap keep this one? She's a lovely kitten."

"No, thank you," said Richard's mother. "I think we'll just wait and see if our own kitten doesn't turn up." So the old lady put

« 18 »

the black kitten back into her shopping-bag and went on down the street.

They had hardly got the door closed when the telephone rang again. This time it was a man who had dachshunds for sale, and he was quite cross with Richard's mother for not wanting to buy any.

And still there was no Mittens.

Again the doorbell rang. Two little girls stood on the porch. One of them held a sad-eyed mother cat in her arms, and the other had a market-basket of very new kittens.

"Is this the cat your little boy lost?" asked the child with the mother cat.

"No, indeed it's not," said Richard's mother in a tired voice.

"Oh, that's all right," said the little girl, cheerfully, "Our mother said to tell you that you are perfectly welcome to all of these cats, because we don't need 'em."

"That's very kind of your mother, I'm sure," said Richard's mother, firmly, "but we don't need them, either." So the two little girls took their cats and went on down the street.

All day long people kept coming to the door with cats. Richard had not known before that there were so many cats in the whole world.

There were little cats, big cats, fat cats, and thin cats. There were black cats, white cats, red cats, yellow cats, gray cats, and brown cats. And if there were any such thing as green, purple, or sky-blue cats, there would certainly have been some of them, too.

But not one of them was Mittens.

CATS
THAT

WEREN'T

MITTENS

All day long Richard thought about little Mittens, lost out in the great world, and maybe cold and hungry and chased by dogs. By dinner-time that night he was so sad he could hardly finish his custard.

"Never mind, darling," said his mother, "if Mittens doesn't turn up tomorrow we'll get you a new kitten."

"But, Mother," said Richard, miserably, "I don't want a new kitten. I just want Mittens." And a tear slid off the end of his nose and splashed onto his last bite of custard.

And then the doorbell rang. It was their neighbor, Mr. Timmons-across-the-street.

"Has the boy found his cat yet?" asked Mr. Timmons.

"No, not yet, Mr. Timmons," said Richard's father.

"Well, there's somebody's cat up in my tree," said Mr. Timmons, "and it sounds like a kitten. Better come over and have a look."

So they all rushed across the street to Mr. Timmons' house, and Mr. Timmons took them out in the back yard to his tree.

"It's too dark to see the cat, I'm afraid," said Mr. Timmons, "but you can certainly hear it."

"*Mew! Mew! Mew!*" came down to them from above. Somebody's cat was up in the tree, mewing as if it would never stop, but Mr. Timmons was right — it was too dark to see it.

"Some dog must have chased it up there," said Mr. Timmons, "and now it doesn't know how to get down."

"Kitty-kitty-kitty," everybody called invitingly, but the cat in the treetop only mewed the louder.

"Oh, Daddy, what are we going to do?" wailed Richard, hopping about frantically.

"I guess we'll have to get a ladder," said his father.

"I have one in the basement," said Mr. Timmons, and he went down and got it. They leaned the ladder against the tree and Richard's father started to climb up it.

"Do be careful, Dick, and don't fall!" warned Richard's mother.

"Do be careful, Daddy, and don't drop the kitten!" warned Richard.

"All right, all right," said his father. And he climbed slowly upward into the dark branches until Richard could see only his legs.

"Kitty-kitty-kitty," coaxed Richard's father, reaching cautiously around in the thick leaves.

"Got him!" he shouted, suddenly, and, "*Ouch!*—you little dickens!" In another minute he was on the ground again with a mewing, struggling scrap of fur in his hand. They looked at it eagerly under the porch light, and—

"*Mittens!*" shouted Richard, joyfully. "Oh, Daddy, it really is Mittens, at last!" He held the kitten tenderly against his cheek and Mittens stopped mewing and began to purr.

Then they all thanked Mr. Timmons and were starting home when Richard thought of something.

"Daddy, what about the reward?" he asked, "You had the paper say there was a reward for finding Mittens."

"That's right," said Mr. Timmons, "and what was that reward going to be, I'd like to know?"

"I think it ought to be about a thousand dollars," said Richard, tucking Mittens under his sweater to keep him warm.

"I'm afraid I can't afford quite that much," laughed his father. "What do you think, Mr. Timmons?"

"I'll tell you what, Richard," said Mr. Timmons. "Supposing you get your mother to ask me to dinner sometime when you are having fried chicken. That would be *my* idea of a reward."

So they invited Mr. Timmons over for the very next Sunday, and after that they went home.

Mittens was so happy to be home again, and to have all the warm milk he could hold, that he purred violently for a long time without stopping. And Richard sat on the floor in front of the fire and petted him, and said over and over:

"Oh, Mother, I'm *so* glad we found Mittens. Aren't *you* glad, Mother?"

"Of course I'm glad, Richard," said his mother, "and so is Daddy. We're all glad. But it is time now for you and Mittens to go to bed."

So Richard put Mittens into his little box and covered him with a piece of blanket. Then he hopped into his own bed and fell asleep thinking happily:

"Tomorrow I'll play with Mittens. And the day after that. And the day after that. And..the..day...after...."

Hand-set in Weiss Antiqua type
by Arthur Rushmore and Faulkner Lewis at the
Golden Hind Press, Madison, New Jersey
1 9 3 6